<u>Dedicated To:</u>
Josie, Andrew, Mike & Jen

<u>Written By:</u> Abigail Gartland

Hello, my name is St. Andrew!

I was a follower of Jesus, and the brother of St. Peter!

When I was a young man,
I started following
St. John the Baptist.

St. John the Baptist was the cousin of Jesus.

St. John the Baptist and I loved spreading the Word of God to all the people we met.

We traveled all over, and St. John the Baptist shared God's word because he knew that his cousin, Jesus, was the Messiah.

St. John the Baptist introduced me to Jesus so I could follow Him, too.

We spent every day praying and serving others.

I spent so much time with Jesus, and I am one of his 12 apostles.

I was even with Jesus at the Last Supper.

I am so thankful for every single day with my friend, Jesus! He believed in me, and helped me to have faith in God.

Do you want to be more like me?

You can celebrate my feast day with me on November 30th

I am the patron saint of fisherman and countries!

St. Andrew, pray for us!

I pray for you every day of your life.

Copyright:

Clipart: © PentoolPixie
Licensed purchased: 1/10/2024

About the Author

Abigail Gartland

I love the saints and I love my faith. The idea for sharing the stories of the saints with little ones came when my dear friends were expecting their first baby. I wanted to create something as unique and special as our friendship. Each book is dedicated to very special people and groups who have enriched my faith in different ways. I am blessed to write these stories and appreciate the unending support of my family and friends. When I am not writing, I am a middle school teacher. I hope you enjoy these stories. I pray for each and every person who opens one of my books to learn more about the saints.

Abbie

www.ingramcontent.com/pod-product-compliance
Lightning Source LLC
LaVergne TN
LVHW051042070526
838201LV00067B/4895

ISBN 979-8-8692-1260-3